WHY DO WE WEAR CLOTHES?

Written and illustrated by

HELEN HANCOCKS

Every day we wake up with things to do, people to meet and places to go.

BUT WHAT TO WEAR ?!

When you get dressed in the morning, how do you decide which clothes to put on?

Perhaps you always put on your favourite shirt or jumper, or maybe you have to wear a uniform, or do you have to dress for a special occasion that requires a fancy outfit?

There are so many things to consider! Do you take a look out of the window to see what the weather's like? Do you need to wrap up warm, or keep cool? Do you want to stand out from the crowd? Maybe you throw on the first things you can find – or do you plan an outfit the night before?

What you wear can say an awful lot about what you are like, what you do, where you come from and who you are.

SO WHY DO WE WEAR THE CLOTHES WE WEAR?!

DRESSING FOR THE DAY

MOCCASIN SHOES

North America

BOWLER HAT

England . . . to Bolivia and Peru!

WHERE in THE WORLD ARE YOU?

Many items of clothing, outfits or fashions are associated with the country traditions or culture where they were first worn – even when no one wears them any more. As people move around the world, these traditions move with them and new ways of wearing clothes are developed . . . But the clothes we wear today may still say something about our ancestors, culture or religion . . .

KILT

Scotland

KEFFIYEH

Middle East

COLOURED BEADS

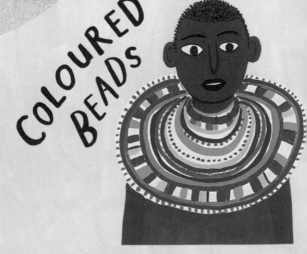

Maasai people of Kenya and north Tanzania

KOLT

Sami people of northern Scandinavia and Russia

SARi

India

GHO

Bhutan

KiMONO

Japan

COiFFE HATS

Brittany, France

GUA

China

And it's not just your country's culture that can affect what you wear.
Have you checked the weather forecast?

WHATEVER THE WEATHER

It's best to know what the weather's like before you get dressed to make sure you'll be properly attired.

Wrap up with plenty of warm layers against that chilly winter wind.

Even snowmen have to dress for the weather!

How about a coat and shoes for your pup?

Or keep cool and
shaded in the summer heat.

The
ice cream
is optional!

LET'S TAKE A RAIN CHECK!

Umbrellas were invented over 4,000 years ago.

On rainy days, umbrellas help to keep us dry.

On a hot and sultry day, you may prefer to shade yourself with a parasol - perfect for promenading!

The 'mac' or mackintosh raincoat is named after its Scottish inventor, Charles Macintosh. A genuine mac is made with rubber-laminated fabric.

SPLISH, SPLASH, SPLOSH!

Gosh! Mary Quant designed some bright galoshes like these in the 1960s.

Once you're kitted out, you'll be dripping with style and singin' in the rain!

WATCH OUT! MOVE ASIDE! EVERYONE HAS *SOMEWHERE TO GO!* THEY'RE ALL IN A **RUSH** TO GET TO WORK (OR SCHOOL).

Can you tell which jobs these people do from what they are wearing?

Some
people
have to
wear a
tie to go
to work or
school. Do you?
Did you know
that there are over

EIGHTY -FIVE

ways to tie a tie?
Just be sure you
don't tie yourself
in knots over it!

In Europe, different sorts of ties have been worn on and off since Roman times. In the seventeenth century, Croatian soldiers wore scarves around their necks to keep their shirt collar fastened. Later, the French adopted this fashion and called the scarves 'cravats'.

SCARF

CRAVAT

BOW TIE

If you want something just as exquisite but a little easier to wear, maybe consider a lacy collar.*

LACY COLLAR

OOOH. FANCY!

For more information on ruffs, see page 43

......AAAND RELAX

You might not be working, but your clothes are! Technology has helped us to produce summer clothes that are thin, light and breezy to wear, unlike this diver's woolly swimming costume!

Many of the outfits we relax in were originally designed for sport, but nowadays lots of us wear sports clothes even when we aren't doing any exercise, because they're so comfy and easy to move around in.

Did you know that if you play tennis at Wimbledon you have to wear white from head to toe? Even your underwear must be white!

Speaking of undies, we need to make sure we're wearing the right thing on our bottom layer. Underwear is usually unseen but it shouldn't be forgotten - it performs some important tasks. Our undies can be used as an extra layer to keep warm; at the same time they prevent the rest of our clothes from getting dirty, and they can give us support too.

Bras, briefs, pants, pantaloons, socks, vests, thermals, long johns, corsets and crinolines - what's your favourite item of underwear? Or do you prefer to go commando?

If we want to make a really big impact with our outfit, we might need some really big underwear to go underneath.

In the mid to late nineteenth century many women wore crinoline cages like this under their dresses: they kept the dress off the dirty floor, shaped the body and supported the weight of the material. However, over time they did get a bit over the top* and were probably rather heavy to carry around!

DOES THIS MAKE MY BUM LOOK BIG?

To see the full effect of a crinoline cage, take a look at the Mantua dress on page 38

Before you head out to start your day you need to make sure you have something on your feet.

...SO FIND A SHOE THAT FITS...

...DANCE AWAY THE BLUES IN THESE...

...MAKE AN IMPRESSION...

...STAND TALL...

...AND PUT YOUR BEST FOOT FORWARD!

21

Be sure to top your outfit off in style with a HAT! They can be functional, or splendiferously silly.

But what is the point of wearing something to be seen in if you can't see yourself?

The first eye glasses were probably made in Italy, and worn by
monks and scholars to help them read and write.

Nowadays there are all sorts of glasses: shades, safety goggles,
flying goggles, opera glasses, monocles.

Bifocals let you see through two different strengths of lens in one pair of glasses, and
were worn by a founding father of the United States of America, Benjamin Franklin.

That's better: you can see clearly now.

WHAT'S IN THE BAG?

A bag is a useful item if you are carrying things about, and it can also be just the right thing to finish off an outfit.

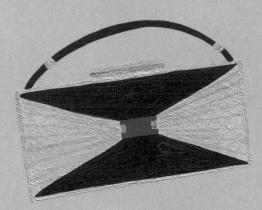

There are **BIG** bags and small bags,

bags for your dog,

bags for your bread,
fresh from the baker's . . .

bags to take
you places,

bags to dance around,

bags for your hat,

bags for small items like
coins or keys, and a bag for
EVERYTHING you need.

WHAT DO YOU CARRY IN YOURS ?

AAAAAA-CHOOOOOOOOOO!!!

If you have the sniffles, you may want one of these.

Handkerchiefs are for more than nose-blowing, though: a hanky can double up as a hat for the beach, a bandage, or a way of getting attention from afar. You can use a handkerchief to signal the start of a race, or to send as a private message to your secret admirer.

 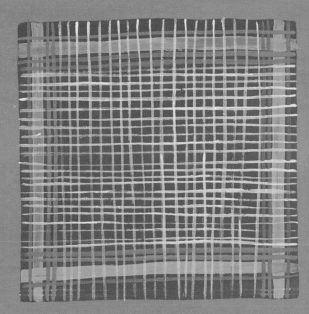

At one time no one in the French royal court was allowed to have a hanky bigger than the king's!

On second thoughts, these handy hankies are MUCH too pretty to use on your nose!

THROW DOWN
THE GAUNTLET…
AND PICK UP A
PAIR OF GLOVES

And if you want a finishing touch to add function or style to your outfit, you might want to pick up one of these . . .

ARE YOU A FAN OF THE FAN?

DRESSING TO IMPRESS

Clothes, as we have seen, can tell us many things about the people who wear them: where they come from or where they are going. But people can also wear clothes to tell others something about their beliefs and opinions. Members of political groups, or protestors, might wear certain clothes to express their thoughts about something to the world.

And sometimes people wear a subtle item of clothing to secretly pass messages to others.

iCONS

DAVID BOWIE

CHARLIE CHAPLI[N]

BEYONCÉ

IRIS APFEL

PRINCE

COCO CHANEL

FRIDA KAHLO

AUDREY HEPBUR[N]

With a specific look or outfit, or with one item that has become intertwined with their identity, these people have inspired and influenced the fashion choices of people all around the world.

MC HAMMER

MARILYN MONROE

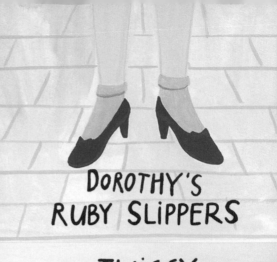

DOROTHY'S
RUBY SLIPPERS

GRACE JONES

YAYOI KUSAMA

TWIGGY

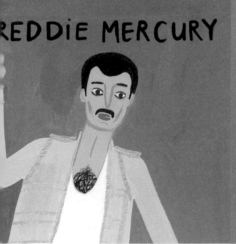

REDDIE MERCURY

JACKIE KENNEDY

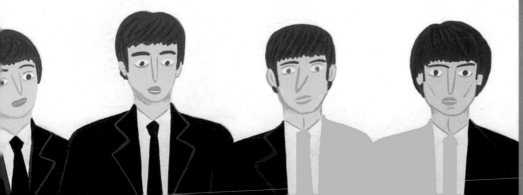

THE BEATLES

MAYBE YOU
WILL BE NEXT
TO SET A
TREND!

A good way to show off your power is to wear something big and imposing, like this Mantua dress, once worn by women at royal courts in France and England. It would have definitely made an impression – it might just have been a bit tricky to fit through the door . . . !

This dress contains over 4.5kg of metal thread – weighing as much as an average cat!

And it's not just the ladies who used their outfits to show off. King Louis XIV of France was a very lavish dresser who thought that clothes were for more than wearing. He used extravagant fashion to show everyone that he was King.*

For an example of this, see over the page!

Did you know that your shoes can say a lot about how important you are? If you were a favourite of King Louis XIV of France, he would allow you to wear red-heeled shoes, so everyone could see who was popular at court.

COURT SHOES

The red heels also made their wearers aware of cleanliness – if you couldn't see the red heel, you needed to clean your shoes!

CHOPINES

Talking of keeping clean, this shoe was designed in Venice to keep feet high above the filthy water that lapped the streets. Over time they became so tall that their wearers needed the help of several servants to walk around.

You might also need help to walk in these shoes . . .

NORITAKA TATEHANA'S HEELLESS SHOES

were inspired by Japanese takagata clogs.

These **VIVIENNE WESTWOOD**

heels were so high that they toppled a supermodel on the catwalk.

Perhaps putting fashion over function isn't always for the best!

If you need to show your status, an impressive hat can help you stand tall. That's why monarchs wear majestic crowns. But power dressing isn't just for kings and queens: what we wear on our heads can say a lot about our importance.

MITRE

A mitre is worn by bishops and archbishops in the Church of England.

TOP HAT

Sixteenth president of the United States Abraham Lincoln was said to store his speech notes under his top hat - handy! The hat brought his height to a towering seven feet tall!

HELMET

Japanese samurai soldiers wore these fearsome helmets to scare their opponents in war.

A CROWN MADE OF FEATHERS

This crown from Papua New Guinea is made using exotic bird feathers as well as plant material.

BICORNE

This bicorne hat was worn by Napoleon Bonaparte, emperor of France, to make himself look taller!

And it's not just what you wear on your head that shows your high status. During Tudor times ruffs were the height of fashion. People wore them to keep clean, but they also became an enormous fashion statement for important people.

THE BIGGER AND SiLLIER THE BETTER!

Queen Elizabeth I wore ruffs that were up to a foot wide! A very impressive sight, but they must have made it a little awkward to eat lunch . . .

PLACES PLEASE!

It's curtain up, and everything is ready to play its part, including the costumes.

Whether a performer is a panto dame, a Shakespearean actor, a dancer, a rock star or an opera singer, they will always wear something that enhances their stage presence and helps them to show off their talents.

If you are watching the show,
please turn off your phone and
remove your hat!

It's not just the performers dressing up for a night on the tiles!
You too might want to push the boat out. Perhaps by wearing
a fancy jacket or a stylish hat . . . Just remember to take it off
before the show starts so that everyone has a clear view!

Why not try the opera hat designed by Antoine Gibus?
It's collapsible so you can stow it under your seat - perfect!
Shhh down the front! It's time to sit back and enjoy the show . . .

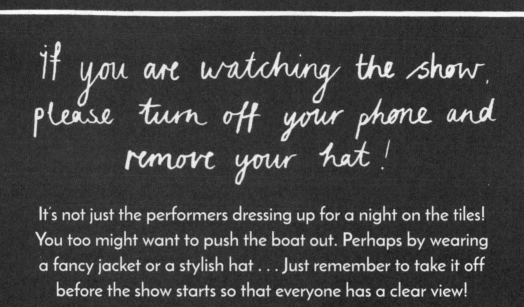

BRAVO!

Look at these shoes - they have danced and pranced all night!

Pointe shoes like these are worn by dancers the world over - but did you know that a pair lasts, on average, for between two and twelve hours' worth of dancing, so some are worn out after a single performance?

A ballet company can get through 6,000 pairs of shoes each year!

OH BOY, THAT'S A LOT OF DANCING FEET!

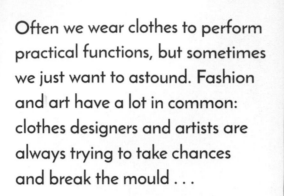

Often we wear clothes to perform practical functions, but sometimes we just want to astound. Fashion and art have a lot in common: clothes designers and artists are always trying to take chances and break the mould . . .

No one put on a show quite like Alexander McQueen! His 1999 collection finale featured robots spray-painting a dress in a wearable art performance.

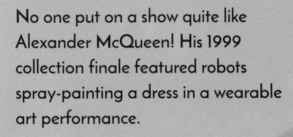

Blimey, take a look at this!
Is it a dress or a table? In 2000
Hussein Chalayan created
a collection of clothes that
transformed furniture into fashion!

Have you ever thought
that a painting looked
good enough to wear?
The designer Yves Saint
Laurent created a dress
that was inspired by the
art of Piet Mondrian.

Fashion designers with a flair for the impressive are inspired by more than high art. Shopping for something to wear can be a feast for the eyes – and stomach!

A PUDDING HAT FOR YOUR LITTLE PUDDING?

For one of your five-a-day, try wearing a basket of fruit on your head like the actress Carmen Miranda – or how about this salad hat?

Elsa Schiaparelli teamed up with surrealist artist Salvador Dalí to create the famous lobster dress. He wanted to smear real mayonnaise on the dress – yuck!

HAVE YOUR CAKE AND WEAR iT!

Did you know that a chef's hat like this is called a *toque blanche*? There are 100 pleats, which symbolize all the different ways to cook an egg – I can only think of five. How about you?!

As we have seen, anything and everything can inspire the design of the clothes we wear, but did you know that the fabrics chosen by designers are also very important? Fabric can transform an outfit and its use, whether you are conquering the extremes of Everest or walking to the shops for milk . . .

Early human clothes were made from what was to hand - like plants - and now technology has increased the material possibilities.

WOULD YOU DARE TO WEAR ANY OF THESE OUTFITS?

Disposable outfits like this one from the 1960s were made out of paper!

This wooden dress might be a little heavy to wear.

This dress is fashioned from silk Second World War army maps.

Fancy a salmon-skin smock?!

This fabric is woven using silk from over a million orb-weaver spiders – eek!

Recycled bottles were used to make this beautiful dress.

What fabrics are your clothes made from?

HOW ABOUT ADDING A SPLASH OF COLOUR TO YOUR WARDROBE!

Well, we have travelled the globe, explored dressing up and dressing down, looked into the whats and whys and hows of the clothes we wear. And now it's time to open up the wardrobe and put some clothes on!

BUT HAVE YOU DECIDED WHAT TO WEAR YET?

WHY DO YOU

IT'S FREEZING OUTSIDE! BRRRR!

I AM GOING DIVING

WE WANT TO LOOK & FEEL GOOD.

'FASHION SHOULD BE A FORM OF OF ESCAPISM & NOT A FORM OF IMPRISONMENT.'

— ALEXANDER McQUEEN

TO STAND TALL!

WE HAVE A SHOW TO PUT ON.

TO STAY COOL & IN THE SHADE

GLOSSARY

FASHION ITEMS:

Moccasin shoes - soft leather shoes, originally worn by Native Americans

Bowler hat - felt hat with a rounded top, popular at varying times in Britain, the North American West and South America

Kilt - knee-length pleated skirt worn as the traditional dress of Gaelic men in the Scottish Highlands

Keffiyeh - traditional Middle-Eastern headdress made from a square cotton scarf

Gua - short jacket, fastened at the side, worn by people in North-East China

Coiffe hats - toweringly high hats made of stiff lace and worn as traditional costume by the women of Brittany, France

Kimono - long-sleeved wide robe traditionally worn by the Japanese for festivals or formal events

Sari - worn by South Asian women, made of lightweight cloth draped so that one end forms a skirt and the other a head or shoulder covering

Gho - a knee-length robe tied at the waist by a cloth belt, this is the traditional dress for men in Bhutan

Kolt - traditional clothing of the Sami people of northern Scandinavia and Russia, featuring bold, contrasting colours and a high collar

Umbrella - hand-held folding canopy used for protection from the rain

Parasol - hand-held folding canopy used for protection from the sun

Galoshes - type of rubber boots that are slipped over shoes to keep them from getting wet or muddy

Tie - long, narrow piece of material, worn around the neck and tied in front; often worn as part of school uniforms or formal business wear

Cravat - wide, straight piece of material worn around the neck, first made popular by the French in the 17th century

Collar - the part of a shirt, dress, coat or blouse that fastens around the neck

Pantaloons - close-fitting trousers that were most popular in the 19th century

Thermals - clothes that have been specially designed to keep you warm

Long johns - close-fitting long trousers, usually worn in cold weather underneath your outer clothes

Corset - a woman's tightly-fitting undergarment that extends from below the chest to the hips, worn to shape the figure and cinch in the waist

Crinoline - full, stiff underskirt designed to hold out a woman's dress or skirt; sometimes a steel cage

Fan - flat, normally folding object you hold in your hand and wave to move the air and make yourself feel cooler

Clogs - heavy leather or wooden shoes with thick wooden soles

Dorothy's ruby slippers - the magic pair of red shoes worn by Judy Garland playing Dorothy Gale in the classic film, *The Wizard of Oz* (1939)

PEOPLE:

Jean Cocteau - French poet, writer, designer, playwright, artist and filmmaker (1889-1963)

Charles Mackintosh - Scottish inventor of waterproof fabric - the Mackintosh raincoat is named after him (1766-1843)

Mary Quant - Welsh fashion designer and British fashion icon (1930-)

David Bowie - English singer-songwriter and one of the world's bestselling music artists, praised for his reinvention and style (1947-2016)

Audrey Hepburn - British actress who was part of Hollywood's Golden Age, recognized as a film and fashion icon (1929-1993)

MC Hammer - American hip-hop artist, known for his flashy dance moves and baggy Hammer pants (1962-)

Marilyn Monroe - American actress, model, singer and popular cultural icon (1926-1962)

Iris Apfel - American businesswoman, interior designer and fashion icon (1921-)

Jackie Kennedy - First Lady of the United States from 1961-1963 and wife of President John F. Kennedy, remembered for her style and grace (1929-1963)

Beyoncé - American singer who rose to fame as part of the R&B girl-group Destiny's Child and is now one of the world's best-selling, most awarded music artists (1981-)

Twiggy - English model, actress and singer known for her signature look of big eyes, long eyelashes and short hair (1949-)

Prince - American singer who sold over 100 million records worldwide and was renowned for his extravagant fashion (1958-2016)

Coco Chanel - French fashion designer and businesswoman who founded the iconic Chanel brand (1883-1971)

Freddie Mercury - British singer, songwriter and record producer, best known as the lead singer of the rock band Queen and for his flamboyant stage persona (1946-1991)

Grace Jones - Jamaican-American singer, songwriter, supermodel, record producer and actress, known for her visual experimentation (1948-)

Yayoi Kusama - Contemporary artist acknowledged as one of the most important living Japanese artists (1929-)

Frida Kahlo - Mexican artist whose work was inspired by Mexico's popular culture and explores themes of identity, gender, class and race (1907-1954)

Charlie Chaplin - English comic actor, filmmaker and composer rose to fame during the era of silent film and is considered one of the most important figures in cinematic history (1889-1977)

The Beatles - English rock band formed in Liverpool in 1960, widely regarded as the most influential music band in history (active 1960-1970)

King Louis XIV - King of France from 1643 until his death in 1715, King Louis XIV was known for his luxurious taste and lavish style (1638-1715)

Queen Elizabeth I - Queen of England and Ireland from 1558 to 1603, her reign is known as the Elizabethan era (1533-1603)

Antoine Gibus - French inventor of the opera hat, a folding top hat that could be stored flat under your seat at the opera (17th century - dates unknown)

Alexander McQueen - British fashion designer who founded a fashion label under his own name and became famous for his dramatic, boundary-pushing designs (1969-2010)

Yves Saint Laurent - French fashion designer who founded the Yves Saint Laurent fashion label, invented the tuxedo suit for women and became one of the foremost fashion designers of the twentieth century (1936-2008)

Piet Mondrian - Dutch painter who was a pioneer in the development of abstract art (1872-1944)

Hussein Chalayan - Turkish fashion designer whose creations mix the human body and clothes with technology, science and architecture (1970-)

Carmen Miranda - Brazilian samba singer, dancer, actress and film star known for her signature fruit hat outfit (1909-1955)

Elsa Schiaparelli - Italian fashion designer whose work was influenced by surrealist artists like Salvador Dalí (1890-1973)

Salvador Dalí - Spanish surrealist artist, most famous for the striking and bizarre images in his work (1904-1989)

Bill Cunningham - American fashion photographer known for his candid street photography (1929-2016)

PHRASES:

Go commando - to not wear underwear underneath your clothes

Throw down the gauntlet - to declare a challenge

Shakespearean actor - someone performing the works of William Shakespeare (1564-1616), an English poet, playwright and actor who is often called the greatest writer in the English language

Credits

Spanning five centuries, the V&A's Fashion collection is the largest and most comprehensive collection of dress in the world. Key items in the collection include rare 17th century gowns, 18th century mantua dresses, 1930s eveningwear, 1960s daywear and post-war couture. The collection also includes a wide range of accessories from across the world, including footwear and hats. Many illustrations in this book were inspired by items in the V&A collection or other existing items of fashion – see if you can recognise them! These items include:

Cover
Pink striped gloves, Elsa Schiaparelli, France, 1937
V&A: T.410&A-1974

Orange paper dress, Diane Meyersohn & Joanne Silverstein, Great Britain, 1967
V&A: T.181-1986

Straw hat, Christy's, Great Britain, mid-1990s
V&A: T.46:5-1997

Silver & black handbag, Unknown, France, c. 1925
V&A: T.238-1982

Yellow kimono, Unknown, Japan, 1930-1940
V&A: FE.32-2014

Dance dress, Unknown, France, c. 1925
V&A: CIRC-14-1969

Pink evening jacket, Elsa Schiaparelli, France, 1937
V&A: T.63-1967

Orange waistcoat, Unknown, France, 1770-1779
V&A: CIRC.516-1928

Embroidered pink tunic, Unknown, Pakistan, 19th century
V&A: T.251-1923

Ostrich feather hat, Oliver Messel, Great Britain, 1939
V&A: S.569-2006

Blue theatre costume, Unknown, 19th century
V&A: S.279-1977

Yellow summer dress, Horrockses Fashions, Great Britain, 1955
V&A: T.11:1 to 3-1997

Red mitten, Unknown, Sweden, 19th century
V&A: 363&A-1882

Green waistcoat, Unknown, China, 1880-1910
V&A: CIRC.33-1936

Blue bathing costume, Jantzen, Great Britain, 1950-1959
V&A: T.113-1999

Yellow & black hat, Unknown, Great Britain, 1930s
V&A: B.13-2016

Green stockings, Unknown, Spain, mid 18th century
V&A: T.156-1971

Page 2-3
Wardrobe, Sir Heal Ambrose, Great Britain, 1932
V&A: W.31:1, 2-1981

Table lamp, designed by George Carwardine & made by Herbert Terry & Sons, Great Britain, 1935-1938
V&A: M.23-2013

Folding screen, 'Bathers in a Landscape', Vanessa Bell & Omega Workshops, Great Britain, 1913
V&A: CIRC. 165-1964

Carpet, Helen Yardley, Great Britain, 1989
V&A: T.87-1989

Pair of slippers, Anello & Davide, Great Britain, c.1970
V&A: T.572:1, 2-1995

Vogue Paris, Condé Nast, France, 1964
V&A: 38041800931438

Black & gold handbag, Rayne, Great Britain, 1989-1990 V&A: T.1208-2017

Green telephone, 'Ericofon 700', L M Ericsson Company, Great Britain, 1976-1980
V&A: W.10-2003

Page 6-7
Kimono, Unknown, Japan, 1920-1950
V&A: FE.145-2002

Pair of moccasins, Unknown, Canada, 1850-1900
V&A: 1172-1903

Moon sari, Suleman & Aziz Khatri, India, 2012
V&A: IS.3:1, 2-2015

Purple jacket, Unknown, China, 1900-1911
V&A: T.5-1911

Page 8-9
Blue coat, T.98-2012, Christian Dior, France, c.1980
V&A: T.98-2012

Brown ski outfit, Unknown, Great Britain, c.1922
V&A: T.241&A-1989

Red ski outfit, Burberry, Great Britain, c.1929
V&A: T.308&A to F-1978

Red jacket, Rajesh Pratap Singh, India, 2009
V&A: IS.25-2012

White & purple dress, The Parachute Collection Elsa Schiaparelli, France, 1936
V&A: T.42:1 to 3-2010

Pink hat, Kilpin Ltd, Great Britain, c.1925
V&A: T.442-1977

Page 10-11
White parasol, Mikhail Evlampievich Perkhin, Russia, 19th century
V&A: T.39&A-1958

Yellow galoshes, Mary Quant, Great Britain, 1967
V&A:T.59:1,2-1992

Red umbrella, Senz°, the Netherlands, 2004-2005
V&A: T.2:1, 2-2015

Green parasol, Unknown, Great Britain, c.1820s
V&A: T.232-1914

Mackintosh raincoat, Hubert de Givenchy, France, 1960s
V&A: T.119&A-1982

Page 14
Ties, Unknown, Great Britain, 1970s
V&A: T.181-1978

Pink tie, Victor Stuart Graham, Great Britain, 1980s
V&A: T.201-1993

Page 15
Lace kerchief, Unknown, Belgium, 1730-1750
V&A: T.263-1922

Collar, Hugh & Florence Baillie Scott, Great Britain, 1903
V&A: T.126-1953

Page 16-17
Green pyjama suit, Unknown, Great Britain, c.1930
V&A: T.176-1967

Yellow bathing suit, Finnegans Ltd., Great Britain, 1937-1939
V&A: T.294&a-1971

Blue silk pyjamas, Unknown, China, 1920s
V&A: FE.3:1 to 3-2013

Smoking suit, Unknown, Great Britain, c.1906
V&A: T.720&A-1974

White linen tennis dress, Great Britain, c.1910
V&A: T.196-1966.

Black bathing suit, Meridian, Great Britain, c.1925
V&A: T.307-1992

Page 18-19
White & burgundy socks, Unknown, Turkey, 1960s
V&A: T.94&A-1990

Green stockings, Unknown, Spain, mid 18th century
V&A: T.156-1971

Blue & white socks, Unknown, China, c.1880-1900
V&A: FE.401:1, 2-2007

Orange stockings, Unknown, England or France, c.1750-1770
V&A: T. 34&A-1969

Page 20-21
Cowboy boots, Unknown, United States, 1940s
V&A: T.600:1, 2-1993

Red pom-pom shoes, Unknown, Turkey, 19th century
V&A: T.181&A-1912

Purple slippers, Unknown, Finland, 1970s
V&A: T.21&A-1981

Brown brogues, John McAffee, Great Britain, c.1925-1935
V&A: T.170&A-1984

Blue boots, Unknown, Great Britain, c.1860s
V&A: CIRC.904&A-1923

Shoes with curled up toe, Unknown, India, c.1800-1900
V&A: 6749(IS)

Chelsea Cobbler shoes, Chelsea Cobbler, Great Britain, 1971
V&A: T.106&A-1974

Silk satin shoes, Unknown, China, 19th century
V&A: FE.78:1, 2-2002

Yellow shoes, Unknown, Great Britain, 1830-1835
V&A: T.178&A-1962

White Superstar trainers, Adidas, Great Britain, 1994
V&A: T.980:1, 2-1994

Red boots, Unknown, Great Britain or France, 1865-1875
V&A: T.180&A-1984

Ballet shoes, Frederick Freed, mid 20th century
V&A: S.796-1981

Tan knee boots, Anton Capek, Vienna, 1895-1915
V&A: T.322&A-1970

Moccasins, Unknown, United States, 19th century
V&A: T.30&A-1954

Snakeskin multi-coloured shoes, Terry de Havilland, Great Britain, 1972
V&A: T.78&A-1983

Blue platform shoes, Biba, Italy, 1972
V&A: T.17&A-1983

Brown Birkenstock sandals, Birkenstock, Germany, 1994
V&A: T.726:1, 2-1994

Toe knob silver sandals, India, 1850-1900
LOAN: CALAM.2:1+2

Page 22-23
Kutch hat, Unknown, India, c.1875
V&A: 0337(IS)

Helmet, Unknown, Korea, 1550-1650
V&A: 118-1878

Buffalo hat, Malcolm McLaren & Vivienne Westwood, Great Britain, 1982
V&A: T.223:4-1991

Knitted hat, Unknown, India, mid 19th century
V&A: 05785(IS)

Shoe hat, Elsa Schiaparelli, France, 1937-1938
V&A: T.2-2009

Quoit turban, Unknown, Pakistan, mid-19th century
V&A: 3462:1 to 8(IS)

Yellow & black felt hat, Unknown, Great Britain, 1930s
V&A: B.13-2016

Embroidered skull-cap, Unknown, India, early 20th century
V&A: IM.28-1912

Nightcap, Unknown, Great Britain, 1600-1624
V&A: T.258-1926

Smoking hat, Unknown, Great Britain, c.1870
V&A: T.198-1968

Page 24-25
Tortoiseshell sunglasses, Oliver Goldsmith Eyewear, Great Britain, 1964
V&A: T.244-1990

White slit sunglasses, Oliver Goldsmith Eyewear, Great Britain, 1968
V&A: T.244B-1990

Red glasses, David Watkins & Wendy Ramshaw, Great Britain, 1966-7
V&A: M.27-2015

Spectacles, Unknown, probably France
V&A: W.5 to B-1970

Triangle sunglasses, Mikli, France, early 1980s
V&A: S.531-1989

Black & gold sunglasses, Stephen Rothholz, Great Britain, 1989
V&A: T.70-2013

Page 26-27
Silver & black handbag, Unknown, France, c. 1925
V&A: T.238-1982

Black & gold handbag, Unknown, France, c.1924
V&A: T.236&A-1972

e House handbag, Lulu Guinness,
at Britain, 1998
A: T.418:1 to 3-1998

broidered cream workbag, Unknown,
gland, 1701-1702
A: T.166-1984

en beaded bag, Unknown, France, 1920s
A: T.189-1997

ite pocket book, Unknown, Italy, c.1700
A: T.29-1915

d lacquer hat case, Unknown, Korea, 1880-1910
FE.1852:2-1993

njara bread bag, Unknown, India, 20th century
A: IS.168-1984

low purse, Unknown, China,
h century-20th century
A: FE.10-1979

tchel, Unknown, Great Britain, 1930-9
A: MISC.81-1990

nged boots, Jim O'Connor & Mr. Freedom, Great
tain, 1970
A: T.709&A-1974

ge 28-29
ppy shirt, Ossie Clark & Celia Birtwell,
eat Britain, 1968-1970
A: T.192-1997

ue & white handkerchief, Liberty & Co Ltd,
eat Britain, 1930s
A: T.514-1974

p left handkerchief, Caroline Charles, Great Britain,
90-1991
A: T.8-1991

p right handkerchief, Unknown, Pakistan, 1867
A: 4934(IS)

ttom left handkerchief, Unknown, 1960-1969
A: MISC.184:1-1988

ttom right handkerchief, Liberty & Co Ltd, Great
itain, 1935-1939
A: T.293-1976

ge 30
nk evening gloves, Elsa Schiaparelli, France, 1938
A: T.393B&C-1974

otty gloves, Bernard Willhelm, Germany, 2000
A: T.82:1,2-2000

ream & black gloves, Freddie Robins, Great Britain,
97-1999
A: T.620:1&2-1999

ellow gloves, Freddie Robins, Great Britain, 1997-1999
A: T.619:1&2-1999

eige leather gloves, Unknown, Great Britain,
30-1959
A: T.258&A-1979

lack, green, yellow & red gloves, Unknown, France,
te 1960s
A: T.916:2-2000

ream patterned gloves, Mary Morris & Charles
icketts, Great Britain, c.1899
A: T.71&A-1939

rey woolen gloves, Michiko Koshino, Great Britain,
93-1994
A: T.395:1, 2-1993

heepskin gloves, Unknown, Europe, 1960-1995
A: T.277:1, 2-1996

d flower gloves, Lesley Slight, Great Britain, 1979
A: T.266&A-1983

ark brown gloves, A. Bide, France, 1910s
A: T.79&A-1960

Red & gold gloves, Unknown, Spain, 16th century
V&A: 437&A-1892

Light brown gloves, Bernard Newman, USA, 1936
V&A: S.1699:1 to 2-2015

Page 31
White fan, Unknown, India, 19th century
V&A: 9797 (IS)

Black feather fan, Unknown, Hong Kong,
20th century
V&A: FE.219-1995

Black & gold fan, Unknown, 1800-1825
V&A: W.5-1944

Red & blue fan, Duncan Grant & Omega Workshops,
Great Britain, 1913
V&A: CIRC.260-1964

Green & gold fan, Unknown, Italy, 1620s
V&A: T.184-1982

Page 34-35
Commemorative Suffragette silk scarf,
Great Britain, c.1910
V&A: T.20-1946

Purple dress, Mascotte, Great Britain, 1911-1912
V&A: CIRC.643-1964

Page 38-39
Mantua dress, Magdalene Giles & Madame Leconte,
England, 1740-1745
V&A: T.227&A&B-1970

Court outfit, Unknown, France, 1790-1800
V&A: T.148 to B-1924

Page 40-41
Blue platform shoes, Vivienne Westwood,
Great Britain, 1993
V&A: T.225:1, 2-1993

Red shoes, Noritaka Tatehana, Japan
V&A: FE.34:1, 2-2015

Page 42-43
Mitre, A.W.Pugin, Great Britain, c.1848
V&A: T.300&A-1989

Samurai helmet, Yoshihide, Japan, 1700-1800
V&A: FE.11-2009

Page 44-45
Tutu, Sir Osbert Lancaster, Great Britain, c.1970
S.1598-1982

Kabuki actor print, Toyokuni I Utagawa, Japan, c.1810
V&A: E.4829-1886

Page 46-47
Purple hat, Woolland Bros., Great Britain, 1910
V&A: T.106-1960

White feather hat, Woolland Bros., Great Britain,
1908-1910
V&A: CIRC.650-1964

Peach feather hat, Aage Thaarup, Great Britain, 1950s
V&A: T.256&A-1985

Page 48-49
Yellow, red & white Mondrian cocktail dress
Yves Saint Laurent, France, 1965
V&A: T.369-1974

Page 50-51
Dame Edna's Breakfast Dress
Stephen Adnitt, Dominic Murray, Mathilde Willis &
Megastar Productions Ltd., Great Britain, 1997
V&A: S.3400-2015

Broad bean salad hat, Deirdre Hawken,
Great Britain, 2010
V&A: T.1-2011

Wedding cake dress, Anthony Holland,
Great Britain, 1979
V&A: S.546-2000

Blue check dress, Hubert de Givenchy, France, 1960s
V&A: T.118-1982
The Souper Dress, Purchase, Isabel Schults Fund
and Martinand Carol Horwitz and Hearst
Corporation Gifts, USA, 1996-7
Metropolitan Museum of Art: 1995.178.3

Page 52-53
White, red & black pattern, Lucienne Day,
Great Britain, 1953
V&A: CIRC.387-1953

Red, black & purple circle pattern, Rosemary Newsom,
Great Britain, 1968
V&A: E.5090-1968

Yellow, white & pink geometric pattern, Lucienne Day,
Great Britain, 1969
V&A: CIRC.39-1969

Green, black & blue pattern, Edward Hughes,
Great Britain, 1955
V&A: E.1399-1979

Rainbow pattern, Susan Collier, Sarah Campbell,
Collier Campbell & Christian Fischbacher,
Switzerland/Great Britain, 1983
V&A: T.185-1984

Teal shapes pattern, Lucienne Day, Great Britian, 1951
V&A: T.329:3-1999

Blue & green paper dress, Diane Meyersohn, Joanne
Silverstein & Dispo, Great Britain, 1967
V&A: T.176-1986

Salmon coat, Unknown, Siberia, c.1900
V&A: 626-1905

Citrus pattern, Maija Isola, Finland, 1956
V&A: CIRC.659-1956

Wooden dress, Yohji Yamamoto, Japan, 1991-2
Metropolitan Museum of Art: 2010.396a, b

Page 54-55
Cream & floral wedding coat, Richard Cawley &
Andrew Whittle, Great Britain, 1970
V&A: T.26-2006

Blue-bordered silk scarf, John Whyatt, Liberty & Co.
Ltd., 1979-1980
V&A: T.74-1985

Pink striped gloves, Elsa Schiaparelli & Salvador Dali,
France, 1937
V&A: T.410&A-1974

Blue patterned top, Unknown, China, c.1880-1920
V&A: T.124A-1961

Striped suit, Mr. Fish, Great Britain, 1968
V&A: T.310&A-1979

Blue & red trousers, Vivienne Westwood,
Great Britain, 1980s
V&A: T.254:1, 2-1991

Blue boots, Unknown, Great Britain, 1851
V&A: T.268&A-1963

Pink fan, Unknown, China, 1950-1988
V&A: FE.209-1995

White wedding shoes, Unknown, Great Britain, 1865
V&A: T.43B&C-1947

Silver boots, Unknown, Great Britain, 1970-1974
V&A: T.61:1, 2-1994

Orange daisy dress, Unknown, Hong Kong/San
Francisco, 1960-1970
V&A: FE.53-1997

Butterfly sunglasses, Oliver Goldsmith Eyewear, Great
Britain, 1950s
V&A: T.243J-1990

Black & white brogues, Unknown, Great Britain,
1920-1940
V&A: T.20&A-1983

Red & yellow shoes, Utility, Great Britain, 1940s
V&A: T.21A-1979

Teal bikini, Coopers, Great Britain, 1983
V&A: MISC.445:1-1984

White trousers, Unknown, Great Britian, 1810-1820
V&A: T.41-1986

Pink evening jacket, Elsa Schiaparelli, Great Britain,
late 1937
V&A: T.63-1967

The Shannongrove Gorget collar, Unknown, Ireland,
800BC-700BC
V&A: M.35-1948

Black wing shoes, Coxton Shoe Co. Ltd,
Great Britain, c.1925
V&A: T.59-1996

Green top, Prada, Italy, 2007
V&A: T.122:1,2-2016

Purple shoes with gold heel, Johnny Moke,
Great Britain, 1990
V&A: T.213&A-1990

Qipao, Unknown, Hong Kong, 1946-1956
V&A: FE.50-1997

Page 56-57
Wardrobe, Sir Heal Ambrose, Great Britain, 1932
V&A: W.31:1, 2-1981

Page 58-59
Boiler suit, Jim O'Connor & Mr. Freedom, Great
Britain, 1970
V&A: T.217-1974

Bathing costume, Viking, Great Britain, 1925-1929
V&A: T.93-1994

Le Bal theatre costume, Giorgio de Chirico, c.1929
V&A: S.851-1980

Find out more about all the
V&A objects featured in this
book at www.vam.ac.uk

PUFFIN BOOKS

UK | USA | Canada | Ireland | Australia | India | New Zealand | South Africa

Puffin Books is part of the Penguin Random House group of companies whose
addresses can be found at global.penguinrandomhouse.com.

www.penguin.co.uk   www.puffin.co.uk   www.ladybird.co.uk

First published 2019
001

Copyright © Victoria and Albert Museum, London, 2019
Written and illustrated by Helen Hancocks
The moral right of the author and illustrator has been asserted

Printed in China
A CIP catalogue record for this book is available from the British Library

ISBN: 978-0-141-38760-4

All correspondence to: Puffin Books, Penguin Random House Children's
80 Strand, London WC2R 0RL